Roddy Teapot

Story and original design by Ian Allen

Adapted from the Thames Television series featuring the Playboard Puppet Theatre

Puppets and Settings by John Thirtle

A Thames Magnet Book

Vanilla has brought Egbert to spend the day with the Spoon family. She is going off to work. Mrs Spoon is very happy to look after Egbert. Egbert and Tina can play together. Egbert wants to know where Mr Spoon is. Tina tells him that her Dad is in the garden shed.

Mr Spoon is busy making a go-kart for Tina. She is asking him whether the go-kart is finished yet?

No, he has still to put the wheels on. Tina tells him that her Mum has promised to take her and Egbert to Button Moon. Mr Spoon watches from the window of the garden shed as the spaceship takes off. 5. . . 4. . . 3. . . 2. . . 1. . . Blast off!

Egbert likes travelling in the spaceship and watching the shooting stars. Suddenly a tea set flies past the spaceship window. Mrs Spoon thinks that is very strange. She has heard of flying saucers, but flying *cups and* saucers . . .! Whoosh! They fly past the window again.

Mrs Spoon can see a kitchen dresser on Button Moon. The cups and saucers are whizzing back to their place on the shelves. Egbert thinks they have been practising their flying. Tina asks her Mum if they can see what else is on the kitchen dresser.

The spaceship lands safely on Button Moon. They all climb out. They can hear the cups and saucers rattling on one of the shelves of the dresser. They make so much noise that they wake up the two mugs, Arthur and Martha Muggins, who live below them. Martha screams, 'I do wish you cups would keep quiet!'

The cups are jumping up and down telling everyone the sad news. Roddy Teapot has lost his lid. He is hiding under the tea cosy. The cups and saucers say they have been flying around Blanket Sky, but cannot find the teapot lid anywhere.

Mrs Spoon tells them they will help look for Roddy Teapot's lid. Roddy lifts the tea cosy, sticks out his spout, and says rather shyly, 'Thank you.' Tina looks in the open kitchen drawer, but all she can see is a tea cloth and a ball of string.
Martha notices something move behind the cheese.

'It has a pink nose, pink ears and a long pink tail,' she says.

'My love, that is a mouse,' says Arthur. Egbert sees the mouse running away as well. Mrs Spoon says they will follow it.

Tina sees the mouse run across the table. Then Queenie Jelly spots it running down the table leg.

'Oh, no!' she cries. 'Not that mouse again!' and she wobbles and shakes so much that some of her cherries drop off!

Jam Doughnut does not see anything. She is too busy bouncing up and down in the sugar bowl, covering herself with sugar. The Gingerbread Men do not see anything either. They are busy practising their handstands. But one of the Butterfly Cakes sees where the mouse went.

Queenie Jelly is delighted: 'Oh, how splendid! Butterfly Cake, you have my permission to leave the table. Hurry and follow that mouse . . . and be careful not to drop any crumbs on the way!' Mrs Spoon, Tina and Egbert go as well, to see where the Butterfly Cake will lead them.

Martha Muggins says, 'That poor mouse! His home must be so draughty without a door.'

Arthur replies, 'Look, I've found one of last year's Christmas cards in the kitchen drawer. He can use that as a door.' 'Eek, eek!' The mouse is delighted. Now he can wish his visitors 'Happy Christmas' all the year round!

Mrs Spoon, Tina and Egbert say goodbye to their friends on the dresser and walk back to the spaceship. Tina wonders if her Dad has finished the go-kart yet. Egbert asks Mrs Spoon if they have to go home yet? No, there is time to look through the telescope first.

Through the telescope, they can see Pamela Pig. She has just given birth to some baby piglets. She has called the first piglet Snort – because he snorts. The second little piglet is called Grunt – because he grunts. The third little piglet is called Curly Tail – because he has got a long curly tail!

Daisy the Cow cannot wait to see Pamela's new piglets. She loves to see all the new-born animals on the farm. Tom the Farmyard Cat wants to meet the piglets too. They woke him up early this morning with their grunting and snorting and squealing!

Peggity the Little Red Hen has not seen Pamela's new piglets. She has not even heard Pamela's new piglets! She is too busy having a morning scratch, clucking and strutting around the farmyard looking for worms. She hasn't even noticed all the grunting and snorting and squealing of the baby pigs!

As it is such a nice day, Pamela Pig has decided to go for a walk and show the piglets around the farmyard, so that they can learn about farm life. She tells them all to keep together. She does not want any of them to get lost. So off they trot.

Pamela Pig shows the piglets where the horse lives. They never see much of the horse because he usually stands out in the field. Then they see a tractor. Pamela tells them never to play near the tractor: it can be dangerous. It's the first time the piglets have been out, so Pamela does not want to go on a long walk. She turns for home. They all trot off together, except one – Curly Tail! He is very tired after his trip trotting around the farmyard. He wants to have a nap in the freshly cut hay.

All that sticks out is his pink, curly tail. Peggity, the Little Red Hen, cannot find any worms. Suddenly, she sees the tail, but she thinks it is a worm. She gives it a peck. There is a squeal, and up jumps the piglet. Peggity has such a surprise!

Pamela Pig comes looking for Curly Tail. Peggity explains that she is sorry, but she didn't know that Pamela had any piglets. And Curly Tail has learnt his lesson! He will never run off again.

Egbert liked watching the baby piglets through the telescope. Mrs Spoon says it is time to fly home: Egbert's Mum will be waiting for them. They all climb into the spaceship and get ready for the countdown. 5. . . 4. . . 3. . . 2. . . 1. . . Blast off!

The spaceship travels fast through Blanket Sky. Mrs Spoon can see their house from the spaceship window. Egbert asks whether she can see his Mum. Mrs Spoon says she cannot. Vanilla might be indoors.

They get closer and closer to home, then Mrs Spoon presses the round button, and the spaceship lands safely in the garden.

They climb out of the spaceship just as Egbert's Mum arrives from work to pick up Egbert. At the door of the cardboard-box house, Mr Spoon is waiting with the go-kart he has made for Tina. Egbert would love to have a ride in it, but his Mum says, 'Not today. It is time to go home. Egbert has done enough travelling for one day!'

This Magnet edition first published in Great Britain 1984 by Methuen Childrens Books Ltd
11 New Fetter Lane, London EC4P 4EE
in association with Thames Television International Ltd
149 Tottenham Court Road, London W1P 9LL
Reprinted 1986 (twice)

Book design by Sue Ryall
Roddy Teapot 0 423 01260 6
Printed in Great Britain